Tammy L. Swank

Sequoyah Road

American Prose

Sequoyah Road, American Prose
by Tammy L. Swank

First Edition

Distributed by Lulu.com

Dedicated to Terri Lynn:

We were wild as the flowers we picked.
Thank you for a lifetime of inspiration.

American poetry "Aims to define whatever is truly indigenous and unique in the American tradition itself."
-Prof. Henry W. Wells University of Columbia

Contents	Form	Page

Preface

Sequoyah Road *is a point of departure, a new voice lending strength to seek and to find. This collection strives to embark on an exploration of the simple pleasures and struggles of rural Americans. It celebrates ordinary people surrounded by the beauty of nature. Its purpose is to reform our thoughts through the stimulation of soulful wandering. It reminds us to reconsider the familiar things and bring us home with a new perspective.*

Poetry is unique within the arts. It has literary content yet it is a living, breathing thing. A poem is composed from the formalities of language, but it is set apart from ordinary writing. It is the poet's responsibility to relay a feeling from the most passionate portion of his mind with the best possible words and mechanics of written language.

Although I have studied the master poets and have been a student of literature all my life, I found a particular approach to creating this book. It has been greatly inspired by the writings of Henry David Thoreau, especially the Walden Woods Project for its fearlessly detailed accounts of a singular life in the wild. It is a remarkable and vigorous search for solutions and social conscious through an insatiable love for nature.

After moving to the farm eight years ago where most of my neighbors are cattle and horses, I found myself immersed into a wholesome life with humble surroundings. Along with plenty of peace and quiet, I am able to enjoy healthy well water, fresh eggs and a wood burning stove. I can grow my own vegetables and hang clothes on a line if I choose.

This all lends to my independent personality and pioneering spirit. I do not need to wander off into the woods forever, but it is nice to know I could. Writing pastoral poetry inspired by these times on the farm gives me immense satisfaction. It is my hope that the following collection be revered for a sense of honesty, nostalgia and rustic quality.

I would like to thank my daughter, Carolyn Claussen who always helps edit my work. Thanks to the thousands of people who have viewed my page on Poetry Soup. It really keeps me going.

This book may be read anywhere that poetry lives. It may be consumed in small bits or in whole. Take it with you so you may have it at the coffee shop or while you are waiting for a hair appointment. Read it when vacationing in the wide open of a state park. Keep it for long rainy days snuggled in bed. Enjoy it all the way to the end and then read it again.

Good Morning, America!

It was a long lonely night at the lumber mill
Just listening to a whippoorwill
In the dark beside a logging road.
I've got fifteen cars of timber on my load.
The yard stinks of bleeding sap and cut pine.
Roll on, roll on down the line.

I'll be on my way before the dawn
Through the bottoms and the swamps.
Before first sun light on the timber lot,
Backwater sloughs and cypress knots.
On rusted rails I'll be making time
When the horizon winks a thin gold line.

I'll be rumbling down this long steel track,
Somewhere between porch light and pitch black
While coyotes call out for the night.
My engines will be roaring around the bend
As the night bird's song comes to an end.
Roll on, morning train, roll on.

Then day break will lay on morning dew,
As the logging town fades out of view.
I'll give my whistle a blow, blow
To make the farmer's rooster crow.
By the time the sun has warmed me,
Old men will be drinking their coffee
As I roll through the station.

I ask you leave an open car
For misty eyed hobos and runaways.
Let them know the clotheslines, highways,
And countless telephone poles.
Sunshine and shadows clicking time
Beside the graveyards, grain silos,
And other lonely places.

They'll be greeted by multitudes of sparrows,
Smiling house wives in their bathrobes,
Unwashed cars and graffiti
Behind the back yards of society.
They'll find comfort in the rhythm of the day
Beside the dusty dirt roads and alleyways.
Roll on, big freight train, roll on.

The American Pioneer

The American pioneer is tough,
Thick-skinned with great inner strength.
He knows that life is both
Deep and fragile.

The American pioneer is courageous.
He knows that 'going against the grain'
Is not an easy prospect. All the while
Nature presses against his weak fortitudes.

The American pioneer lives by necessity.
He does not attach himself
To communities of opinion
Who arm against the world.

Rather, distances himself
From the spoils of civilization,
Lest he be down-graded.

The American pioneer is not preaching
On the minimalist way,
Nor complacent on the issues of the day.
But focused on the methods of attainment
And how much one can accomplish.

The American pioneer is always striving
For something different.
Maybe curiosity gets the better of him.
He bows his chest and pushes back
The untamed land.

The American pioneer struggles
For the better foothold.
With all his brilliance and aspirations
He turns away from the self-inflated:
The true savages
With their exaggerated importance.

The American pioneer's soul yearns
To redeem itself, to reduce itself
Down to the true measure.
He knows wisdom does not come
By simply letting life happen.

The American pioneer needs to measure his limits,
To try himself into exhaustion
And survive a few winters in this fashion
Until nothing is left untested.

The Early Milking

A new day begins
As the day before.
The Jersey girls assemble themselves
Into their usual cow chain.
One girl's head follows another's tail.
Then head then tail,
All along the sodden trail.
This habit has worn a pasture lane
Of mud and muck,
And cow to barn.
They plod the path with bulging udders
To give sweet milk made from clover.
Lo! It is a ritual
Of back and forth,
To and fro!
The sodden lane is dark as coal.
A sleepy man
Readies himself with pail,
As the girls line up,
First head then tail.
Lo, it is a ritual
Of muffled moos in grain filled troughs
With yellow corn on drooling mouths.
For each cow gets her morning treat
As warm steam rises from the teat.
Woe! A life of barnyard chores!
By hand, he milks
With stool and pail.
Each pet waits her turn in line
By head then tail.
The sleepy bovine moan and snore.
The man, he leans
Against one's side
And rests his head in furry hide.

Such labor,
Grief, care and thought;
Sometimes he thinks to sell the lot.
Lo, barnyard smells invade his dreams
With buttermilk
And warm, sweet cream.
Then big brown eyes meet his in friend.
Come evening,
He will milk again.

Country Dog

If a country dog could talk
        What would he say?
His nose has explored the great outdoors,
        Always smelling unashamedly.
A country dog knows everything,
        So many things he wants to tell you.
There's a brand new colt in the neighbor's barn,
        And baby bunnies in the thicket.
If a country dog could talk
        He would tell you all the things he knows.
There's a row of beans sprouted in the plot.
        Catfish are jumping in the pond,
Where the hedgehog lives down in the bog
        And broken bottles at the old dump spot.
A country dog's knowledge is beautiful.

Morning Prayer

Oh, ye angels of the heavens
Sing praise unto His name
And magnify Him forever.

Bless the Lord,
Maker of heaven and earth,
Of all things visible and invisible,
The maker of the sun and moon,
The showers and dew,
Green things upon the hill.

Oh, ye cattle and beasts
Sing praise unto His name
And magnify Him forever.

Bless the Lord,
Maker of the ice and snow,
Big whales about the waters,
The maker of the seas and floods,
Fire and heat,
All things on this big blue marble.

Oh, ye children of men
Sing praise unto His name
And magnify Him forever.

Bless the Lord,
Maker of humble men of heart.
That they may always incline
To thy will and walk in thy way.
Let the whole earth stand
In awe of Him.

The Birds upon Waking

Why is the ranting outside my window?
Who disturbs my sleep?
Where is the chanting upon my pillow?
What brings the dancing on stick-like feet?
My bloodshot eyes are not open yet,
And circles of laughter above my head.

For a moment, I'll romance the imposing chatter
Before my dreamscape fades.
Then jump to my feet and make them scatter
When dreadful alarm invades.
For shoulder to shoulder, upon a tree limb
They're boasting of freedom in unison.

Then a flurry of wings takes to the sky.
The aerial fit is envisioned from bed
Of sharp beaks and rapid, tiny eyes
Like black, shiny beads on velvet heads.
In plunging dives, a sweet song they sing,
Then banking hard on the curve of a wing.

Bands of tumblers in flawless formation
With swooping emergence have come to feed.
Multitudes more join in participation;
A destructive gorging on the apple tree.
Such a commotion of chirping, feathered beasts
And countless other living things.

The free birds go on with their preening.
On stick legs they're dancing and singing
With all kinds of winged flutter;
A rowdy ruckus up in my tree.
I try to decipher, what is the matter?
I know their concern is not for me.

Breakfast Dishes

Every day we woke up hungry.
We ate our little bowls of freedom
At the breakfast table.
Then Momma washed the breakfast dishes.

In the summer,
Momma grew maters and beets.
She stooped in earnest to keep us fed.
We sopped our shame with bread.
Yellow dishes lay in the sink.

We lived those years without thinking
About leaving the little white house.
The check came once a month.
We pinched our pennies carefully.

The house stood dressed in red shutters
On a street that no one cared about.
Time wore a yellow calm.
Momma's dishes lay in the sink.

In the winter,
We huddled closer to the stove.
Steam grew on the windows,
Fried taters and a pot of beans.
Yellow dishes rattled in the sink.

On the back porch, thin cats waited
For a bite of something worth eating.
They cried at the screen door
While Momma washed the breakfast dishes.

At supper time,
We ate our plates of charity,
Fried bologna and government cheese
With a false sense of peace.
Every night we went to bed hungry.

Ecclesiastes 3:1

To every thing
There is a season
And a time
To every purpose
Under heaven
A time to weep
A time to grow
A time to think
A time to pray
A time to move forward
In His name

The Farmer

The farmer has a dream
To live by his own reign
In humble homestead and great outdoors.
The farmer must endeavor
To survive in God's country
And be satisfied in his prospects.
The fences go up by his hand.
He chastens the feral pastures,
Remember me, 'less they forget his rule.
The farmer lives boldly;
Resistant to the inclinations of man.
It is a practice of self-emancipation.
The farmer has no foes to crush
Nor banners to unfurl.
His focus is on the pertinent.
His interest is a bit of earth,
To raise some stock and herbs.
He wants to live authentically.
The farmer faces nature head on
And embraces his dependency on it.
He knows his plans are tentative.
His hard-won life, a testament,
As he weeds out the world's complexities
And masters the follies of his vocation.

The Woodsman

When thickets blush with staghorn; crimson,
Broad landscapes hint of golden brown.
Tired walnuts cast away their burden,
Black, heavy fruit upon the ground.

Into the woods! For winter's coming.
Autumn, she lasts but for a while.
The woodsman's chest fills with her promise;
Two rick of oak, skies clear and mild.

The air is crisp. The woodlot's waiting
Beyond the reaches of the town.
The way: a tree-lined narrow winding
Of sunlit-dappled, derby brown.

Nests hang listless, unraveled and torn,
Long forgotten amid the brambles.
Beside the road, soft spleenwort fern,
Wild rose hips and thorny tendrils.

Fence row gives way to unmarred meadow,
A rich and temperate estate.
Beyond, the static timbers - yellow.
Oh, seize the day! The woodlot waits.

Into the woods! To fell a fine oak.
Post or Pin? He surveys the stand.
Which wood to cull, Bur oak or Arkansas?
The restless axe weighs in his hand.

He makes his claim among the timbers.
He swings of swiftness, not of haste,
And would not leave someone else to tend.
The cloven logs fall splinter-less.

Lengths of warmth on block divide.
Fat grubs exposed by sapwood crushed.
Loud echoes pierce the countryside
Sending hedgehog to the underbrush.

He loves his work. The task; his pleasure.
With maul and skill, dry timbers crack.
His yield, a load of wood to measure
With pride, admires the handsome stack.

A sign of frost comes on the breeze,
The rustling of the withered leaf.
Winter lies waiting beneath the trees;
A bustle in the underneath.

He rubs his face; red rough with stubble.
Puts down his axe and rests awhile.
Warm calf-skin gloves embrace his thermos,
At peace, alone within the wild.

The Cabin

I came upon a little cabin
While in the woods one late November.
The day had met me in a cusp.
The season lingered in its clove,
For autumn's blush had passed its peak
Yet winter's snow had not set in.

Compelled by unseen force inside.
Began my jaunt with restless stride.
Took path obscure and over hill,
Then pointed my footsteps further still.
To wood lines washed in muted umber:
A fog-swept skirt of shedding timber.

I rambled on where wood line fades
As way lead on to rural way.
Through humble woods and passed the bounds,
Across the stubbed and matted ground.
I found myself, a place remote
While dew had gathered on my coat.

I cleaved the edge of timberline.
The passing alders marked my stride.
When at a glance and in between
By chance, a cabin on the clearing.
I ventured farther than I should
And didn't know this cabin stood.

Whose woods were these?
Tucked in the tangled, palsied weeds,
Where brushstrokes blur amid the trees
In shades of plum from withered leaves.
Whose woods were these?
I did not know.

'Twas by mistake my passing near
For trespassing had brought me there.
A hunter's lodge or hermit's den?
But someone keeping house within.
For windows cast a little light
Through thinning brush with foliage spent.
This rustic cabin caught my sight.

A quaint homestead all nestled in
The rough wildwoods at venture's end.
My purpose there, not to impose.
From out the chimney, a tender rose.
It billowed up in scrolls of blue
To make a charming, stolen view.

Colossians 3:23

And whatsoever you do,
Work at it with all your heart
As to the Lord, and not unto men.

Our days have been stressful and exhausting,
Running on extreme emotion and bad coffee.
We have been offered solace and compassion.
Also, witnessed quiet acts of humanity.
We have been showered with love and kindness.
You have been on our side,
Praying with us and holding our hands.
This experience has humbled me.
Also, filled me with such joy.
You lead with your heart.
For this, I will be forever grateful.

The Robin's Nest

While gathering wood one autumn day
To make a stack beside the stove,
I spied a nest along the way
Of back and forth and to and fro.

November's wind had forced it down.
I took the time to pick it up,
This robin's nest upon the ground,
Then held it gently with my glove.

I looked for answers up in the elm
To see from where it came dislodged.
I held the craft upon my hand,
And spun it round in wonderment.

To weave a cup from twigs so fine,
Stole bits of sage and lavender,
Small tufts of moss and battered twine,
Woolen yarn from an old sweater.

To darn a home with such keen eye
Must be a bird of graceful stock.
Her handiwork beneath the sky
Must earn her praises among the flock.

For holly berries pierced the spray
Of saw tooth grass and tangled weed.
A lofty home with leafy shade
Of downy-tucked and winding reed.

She worked o'er treetop and chimney
To gather many a splendid thing.
She sang a whimsical melody
Of peaceful groves and feathered wing.

Once bright blue eggs had filled this nest
Through starry nights, mid- summer's storm.
All pressed beneath her scarlet breast;
She kept them safe from snare and thorn.

She raised her clutch on branches high
With fitful scorn and lessons shrill.
Then spread her wings to let them fly;
A prideful scarlet bosom swell.

Now autumn's red has left the trees.
Cold winter's breath is on the sill.
The rustling of a withered leaf
Holds no sweet song nor feather quill.

When spring returns on budding leaves
To grace this farm with robin's wing
Thickets will flush with hearts afire
And geese will sift upon the mire.

The earth will thaw as days grow long.
Come May, again I'll hear her song
And all kinds of fluttering about
While turning blossoms inside out.

The robin's work will start again
With tufts of moss and battered twine,
For chance will find her way to me.
A nest, she'll build amid my tree.

Weary Travelers

I saw a thousand geese fly by.
From north to south,
They marked the sky.
Thrown off their course by winter storm,
On hapless and drifting route.
An endless, massive flock
Spanned my view in jagged form.
The fleet looked to be give-out.
And hundreds trailed behind the lead
In long, lop-sided, wavering vies.
Tired yearlings wobbled within the rears,
Beating their wings with mindless fear.
I watched for some to land my pond,
To sift the mire through reed and frond,
But each bird flew with forward breast,
Deprived of strength and pounding chest.

The Buttonwood

One day while wandering with a friend
Down country road to river's bend,
A wooden bridge o'er country mile,
Alone, we sat there for a while.

'Twas in our youth this late September
Two souls took rest above a river,
Where rocks and roots o'er hung the loam
To touch the swirls of turbid foam.

Red leaves held in the runnel's grasp
Slipped on the rills then quickly passed
From bend to bend on winding rush
With waters brink and autumn blush.

Downstream, an elm grove stood rank
Held closely to the rooted bank.
Amass, sent forth their scaly arms
To shade the creek with all their charms.

Amid the bent and shedding yellows,
The faded green of handsome willows,
A massive trunk with ancient growth -
From seed, fast anchored to the earth.

Note a buttonwood in mottled white.
What graced this giant to pious heights?
And rise so high above its peers
To conquer the wind unnumbered years.

For upward, splendid limbs unfurled.
Grey bark gave way to skin of pearl.
Beside the creek, far leaning out,
This buttonwood grew strong and stout.

Even now when wandering nature's trail
By water's edge, through lonesome dale,
Per chance, to see a buttonwood.
What weathered years it must have stood!

Far longer than that late September
And friendships no more remembered.
But glints of broad and palmate leaves
Cast soft reflections on the creek.

Like leaves on rills, they slip on past
Pushed downward by some torrent blast,
Where time has piled the matted ground
With autumn mist and umber brown.

Epistle No. 1

Mom,
Sorry I forgot to give you the rent
When I saw you on Sunday.
Maybe your forgetfulness is contagious.
Maybe it was the Mexican food . . .

Billy and I are really enjoying the house.
Thank you both so much
For all that you have done for us.
You've really saved us.
I don't know where we would be
Without the help and gifts you've given us.

We love you so much,
Billy and Carolyn

Picking Blueberries

We've come from far away
Like all the others.
A morning spent on lonesome dirt roads
Searching for the blueberry farm;
Endless acres of hazy blue groves.
The pickers trickle in.
We step out of our cars
Into the dust with straw hats
To block the blistering sun.
The owner sits on her porch
With stacks of clean buckets
And a chest of cold bottled water.
It is the hottest day of the year.
Dirt and sweat gather on our necks
As we hurry to the shady rows.
It is on sad occasion that we come
To pick the wonderful berries,
Disturbing them from their thickets,
Taking them before their end is due.
The sweetest ones taunt us
Just out of arm's reach.
We are no better than the canker
And worms that kill.
The owner graciously snaps a photo
To mark the day.
We huddle close in goofy grins,
Sun burnt with buckets teaming.

The Tolling Bells

Hear the ringing of the bells.
Wake up! Wake up ye citizens!
Rejoice! Rejoice for ye are saved!

Angelic choir voices swell.
Join in fellowship with ye friends.
Hear the ringing of the bells.

Oh! How I love the tolling bells.
Bewildered hearts our Savior mends.
Rejoice! Rejoice for ye are saved!

When Jesus comes, no one foretells.
On Him your tarnished soul depends.
Hear the ringing of the bells.

In your heart His spirit dwells.
Repent and be free of your sins.
Rejoice! Rejoice for ye are saved!

All weary souls be compelled.
Wake up! Wake up ye citizens!
Hear the ringing of the bells.
Rejoice! Rejoice for ye are saved!

Cold Snap

The first frost came without warning,
Embarking on the brilliant red mulberry.
The only one among the oaks:
Twisted and bent by laborious years.
The woods held fast a solemn silence,
The ground, an unexpected white.
When the tardy sun came creeping
It melted some stiffness away.
Every green leaf was gone.
The remaining foliage shivered
Below October's fitful brow.
Just last summer,
A swollen fruit then mulberry wine.
Now a tired, gnarly centerpiece
Shedding each blood red leaf
One by one.
They begrudged the Earth
That tugged, then floated down.
A soft pitter-patter among the groans;
They gathered below the naked limbs
In shades of Macintosh, grapefruit
And tangerine.

Epistle No. 2

Dear God,
Have mercy on my soul
For I have a daughter.
From birth, such joy this child has brought.
My affections, she has eagerly sought.
Well wishes to this precious child.
In her, the whole world beguiled.

Keep her from the slightest prick.
Never a day may she be sick.
May you, my God, her mind anoint
With wit so sharp be to a point?
Of pretty things she'll ne'er want;
Her little purse be filled with coin.
Dear God,
Have mercy on my heart
For I am a mother.
Bless this girl both fair and bright
To know between the wrong and right.
In circles, it seems she is well-liked.
Her temperament is always mild.
Among her peers she's well respected.
From harm, her heart be close protected.
Her beauty I'm inclined to mention;
A complexion made from porcelain,
And more modesty has ne'er been given
To the angels who abide in heaven.
Her tender face is white as snow
With playful eyes, two shining globes.
May she be fit in velvet robes,
Two golden rings upon her lobes?
May silken slippers protect her feet
That tip-toe light and smell so sweet?
Set her hair in ribbons and myrrh
To lay upon her back in curls.
I pray that she be fitly wed
In gown and ring and joyful bed.
For a halo rests upon her head
And gracious words about her said.
Oh! Fruitful days throughout her life
To be a strong and loving wife.
Someday, a daughter she may bear.
This is my truest, solemn prayer.

Otis Corley's Foible

Oh hail the common man!
He's something of a novelty.
Never has he asked for much.
Some people call him Hillbilly.

Watch, remember, celebrate

His coveralls are washed in lye
Then pinned upon a line to dry.
From rural soil his children sprout.
They're raised on beans and sauerkraut.

Warp, weft, seam and weave

All for peace and love proclaim,
Have mercy on a peaceful man!
Of simple means and meager lot,
He rides with sure and even trot.

Canter, gallop, ambling gait

Though others fail, he finds no fault,
Endures his fate and woes begot.
His portion is at nature's whim.
Long days are spent behind his team.

Summer, fall, wind and rain

He plows his fields in furrows deep
And plants his yams deliberately.
Then digs the yield with hoe and spade
To pace the sun in senseless race.

Winnow, thresh and sow the seed

Next year will bring a better yield.
He keeps his garden neatly tilled.
He bows his chest in hopeful gain,
Then hangs his head and prays for rain.

Struggle, plan, hope and dream

Hay Gathering

He unfolded his chair
In a sliver of shade
On the east side of the barn.
The pink lemonade stung
In the cracks of his blistered lips.
A panting breath
Of wind came by. Cooling the sweat
On the back of his neck.
He gazed off at the flaxen rolls
And dreamt all of them were stacked
In the boiling hot barn.
Quietly, he watched a hay devil
In its whimsical spinning,
As it went about its work
Under the daunting sun.
Lazily circling the field,
Taunting the afternoon
For the remaining dew and
Taking with it the last bit of moisture.
A tumble weed at his feet
Shared the comfort of the shade.

Dust

I need nothing
But the red setting sun
And to rest easy in the palm of night
With the prairie's cool arms around me.
I came in on dirty horse hooves
And lonely cowboys' hats,
Blown far away from the cities
Where houses and bridges rise up.
I say nothing.
Old wooden fences and barbed wire
Can't keep me out,
A scarf tied in a knot at the chin,
For I am in the wind.
You will find me
On children's feet in late summer.
The farmer's wife sweeps me out,
But I creep under her door
And hide in her cupboards.
I am not afraid of the chimneys
With their blue billowing towers.
For I am a bucket of ash in winter.
You have seen me
Lingering over corn fields, tall and upright,
Sticking to tassels and ears.
In the evening hours I am the dusk.
The farmer stuffs his hogs until they waddle.
He hacks them with cleavers
And hangs them on hooks.
I say nothing.
I have been driven out by the axe
That claims the timber
And I bite at the plow.
I cling to the wolf's throat, choking.
It is I who holds all things together.

I was there on dark days
Among the killings of young men.
I was the last survivor
When wars were fought.
I say nothing.
The rain and the sun and the wheat
Have haggled it over.
The rainbow in the east pledges
And the broken well pitcher boasts;
They will wash me away.
I flourish where the old things go,
Covering the writings on head stones.
It is all mine eventually.

Epistle No. 3

Your trunk was open
And it wouldn't shut
With your purse in it.
I took the purse to
Service desk and they
Sent it to security.
I didn't want anyone
To steal your purse.
Merry Christmas

Put your hands together
This is a church
And this is the steeple
These are the doors
And here are the people

Mother

I thought I found you in the blue
Of a tiny broken robin's shell.
I thought I heard you calling me
In the squeaking of a child's swing,
As distant playground voices swelled.
I thought I saw you in the blue,
Glancing sweep of feathered wing.

I searched through faded linens,
Your things in the china cabinet.
I longed for your embrace.
I drove passed the old homestead;
A crumpled foundation in a field.
It was emblazoned with daffodils.
I looked, but you were not there.

I walked the path that winds between
The quiet woods and bubbling spring.
Then stood upon the weathered bridge
And hung my fitful head.
I hoped to see your hazel eyes
In the sun-shade dappled stream,
Where smooth, grey stones lay sleeping.

I searched for strength to climb the hill
And walk among the Who and Who,
Where lichen grows without a sound
Upon the names moored to the ground.
I knelt beside your rose pink stone
And dreamt of June's familiar blooms,
To bring me closer to you still.

The River

The river remembers
When the first man came to drink,
And the ice cold April melt
Of a heavy March snow
That fell a century ago.
It was a narrow, struggling stream
Searching for its way between the hills.
The old river knows everything.
It is full of suffering; toppling
And gnawing at the bedrock.
Its' pummeled banks are punished
With uncountable raindrops
Upon raindrops.
My oar trudges the haunted water.
The old river holds many things,
Dead branches, bones and shadows.
Silent creatures dwell in its' dark swirls.
It holds the misplaced things,
Ray-Bans, fishing lures and flip-flops.
The river is afflicted as a woman's heart;
Keeping its' secrets in the deep
Cold basement of the underneath.
It holds many tears
And wayward spirits that loom
On sleepy layers of river mist.
My oar trudges the turbulent tears.
A rushing torment carries them away.
The old river flows on and on,
Pushing its' burden toward the sea,
And still the river remains.

Big Head

Big Head showed up at the house
One August day when the sun
Had scorched the ground by mid-morning.
He had wandered over from the ball park.
Found his way down the alley
That ran behind the back fence.
His mouth was so dry that
He couldn't swallow.
The pads on his feet were blistered.
Joe sat out a pot of water.
Big Head drank almost all of it.
Then he lay under the porch
In the shade for the rest of the day.
He was pretty much Joe's dog from then on;
A brown and white mix of boxer and pit.
Sometimes he would growl and bear his teeth,
For Big Head's heart never forgot
And it never grew old.
In the cool of the evening
Big Head would start his songs,
Long, slow howls of torment and hunger.
At night he wandered the streets alone
Singing his sad stories,
Conjured from the inmost portion of his heart
Where a mighty love once grew.

Sequoyah Road

Between third and fourth grade
The summer heat crept up to our front door
Without warning
Like a pair of Jehovah's Witnesses.

We didn't care
That Bennie and the Jets was a number-one hit
Or that Gerald Ford was going to be
Our next president.
We spent long golden days
Running and hiding,
Spying on other kids in the neighborhood.
All the houses were the same really;
Different only by the brick and trim colors.
They were spec homes
Built to house blue-collar families.
My folks were just small-town.
Daddy went from town to town
Speaking for Jesus,
Laying his hands on the believers,
Taking away their pains.
We didn't have much, but Jesus flourished.
In the back yard I would swing
As high as I could, then reach out my arms
To test the reality of paradise.
Everybody on Sequoyah Road
Lived on a big Protestant pie crust
That sat right on the edge of the world.
It was the last street on the west side of town.
We were all given strict orders
Not to go past the west border.
There wasn't anything out there anyway,
Just dirt roads and honky-tonks.
That's where people went to get their booze.
It wasn't hard to imagine the Earth
Coming to an end out there somewhere;
Crumbling away into space like a big pie crust.

November

A November wind has roared for days.
Dead garden stalks lay bent and frayed.
The proud maple now stands undressed
In drifts of yellow against the fence.

Broken remnants lay on the yard;
A scattered blast of limbs' discard,
The fallen litter in blissful calm.
A roaring November wind is gone.

The crickets have hushed and gone to sleep.
All nestled beneath the barberry.
While snowbirds busy the hedges to feed
Where ruffling winds misplaced their seeds.

Sadly, the walnut has nothing left to shed,
But an ivy still clings in brilliant red.
A rusted barn roof is left exposed
Where distant arbors used to grow.

And chimneys sew their grey, woolen clouds
For the bleak sky wears a sullied shroud.
The curls of smoke gracefully unwind.
As for me, a pensive knot inside.

To see the snowbird's round, feathered breast,
And to think. Each year uncoils from the next.
Bright leaves that held such hope in June,
I've collected to make a sick perfume.

And piled these treasures in a heap;
Now smoldering and weeping in the heat.
I huddle closer to the crackling flame,
Knowing that winter will come again.

Counting Sheep

It must have been late afternoon.
I could tell by the shadows
Running away from the sun.

He had many sheep, as shepherds often do,
Hundreds of sheep with black noses,
Black hooves heavy under thick coats.

It must have been late autumn.
I could tell it was getting cold.
Our breath clung to the slanting rays.

Coming in from the hills; their numbers grew.
Too many to count, dirty coats in a grey haze,
Shadows stretching out from the sun.

It must have been late afternoon.
The young ones finally finding their way
Stubby tails wiggling, black hooves jumping.

Many sheep were tucking themselves in,
Jumping the fence to get in the barn,
Hundreds of wool coats and black noses.

The Primrose

Dawn let itself in through the barn door.
Its' golden voice made an announcement,
"This is the beginning of summer!"
I sniffed the spring wind for summer's heartbeat.
Rolling hills lifted their shoulders and sighed,
Heavy with green and buttercups abound.
A handful of sparrows cheered the day.
Their tiny tracks marked my way
Beside the mire, fraught with peeping frogs,
As the sun broke free from the clouds.

Then the flash of a mocking bird tail
Drew me across distant, rocky trail
Among the oaks where wild things grow,
A parcel forgotten, untouched.
I stopped somewhere to catch my breath.
Not knowing how far along the path.
To observe, to touch and to see
The rough wildness that beckoned me.
I listened to the peaceful whir
Of the Earth in its quiet spinning.

A location where deer might bed
For the broken trail was rarely tread.
Overwrought in pensive feeling
As lilies near the graveside weeping.
I was alone with the mocking bird.
Quite surprised at my discovery;
A wild primrose in the shady soil,
Up early with the morning ray,
Tucked in beside a litter of leaves,
Held safe from any trampling.

The lady had postured herself
In a beguiling performance
As if she'd seen me coming up the lane.
A dazzling display of yellow petals
Clambering and reaching upwards,
More delicate than a pigeon egg
And precious as hummingbird wings.
"What brings you here?" I asked.
"A seed, fallen from the hunter's cuff
Or brought on the wren's tufted muff?"

How many seasons with no passer's by?
Set alone to rise, bloom, then fade
Never witnessed by a single eye.
Meanwhile, I have wandered the Earth,
Unsettled and searching for what?
While the primrose grew here; wanting not,
Feeling at peace in the wilderness.
For God has made her not afraid
And she has fared better than I;
A happy yellow primrose.

Dog Poem

When you talk to dogs
They really listen.
They are not just waiting
For you to stop talking
So they can say something.
They really listen.

Dogs are like little children really,
Little children that never grow up.
They always want to be cuddled.
All dogs are lapdogs really.

Canned Biscuits

Fried taters and beans,
Beans and fried taters.
The cupboards were bare
By nineteen seventy-six.
My sister in all her droning
Heard a can burst in the fridge.
The leavings; my dad had brought
And swallowed his pride
To fish through the trash
Behind the grocer's store or asked
For a hand-out from a church.
My sister in all her silliness
Proclaimed the biscuits expired.
Tossed the cans out back
To swell in the sun.
The pop, pop, pop
Of exploding cans made her giggle.
And then what,
And then what did we eat?
Beans and fried taters,
Fried taters and beans.

The Gardener's Confession

I think I could stay here
In the garden,
Living among the herbs,
Sleeping in the lavender bed.
There is a profit of companions
To be had.
The rosemary and the mint
Could prove beneficial.
Here is a host of tiny blossoms
To wrap my fingers around.
To be honest,
I like all the eyes upon me,
The tomato's red gaze,
My harem of honey bees;
Their wings a yellow blur.
Watching them hover and probe,
The honey bees' feet in yellow dust.
I could take up bad habits
Like standing motionless in wonder
Watching the fog roll off the pond.
I might get carried away
With the ethics of lady bugs
Or the noble suffering of eggplants.
Time could lose all meaning
Other than four-o'clock blooms.
Long hours thrown away
Counting seeds on a sunflower's face.

Freedom Overspill

My day was spent in beds of flowers,
Clipping and tossing away the chaff.
While spring unfolded into summer;
Sun burnt and bent with aching back,
My dirty fingers were sore and cracked.

I was a slave to both sun and earth.
A long hot morning down on my knees,
Breaking the grass roots' hold from the dirt,
Tending the new growth and pulling weeds.
Then relief came in a sudden breeze.

A few large drops hit the flower bed
Like bombs disturbing the helpless ground.
With a flash, the drops bombard my head,
A barefoot dash to the garden shed.
Then all the others came rumbling down.

I was all alone in the pouring rain
And lingered inside the open door.
Banditti-bang, banditti-bang bang,
Sagging sheets upon the clothesline hang
As steam rose off the old enclosure.

The pounding increased velocity.
My face washed in a blurry curtain.
I closed my eyes and began to drink
The refreshing gush. Devouring
Like a child eating watermelon.

I was free from all impending chores
And couldn't hear if you called my name;
Stranded alone in a hard downpour,
Impervious to all culture wars,
Hidden by the sound of pouring rain.

The People, Yes

We are all the family of man
Whether behind shanty doors or skyscrapers.
We wanted something to be proud of
So we put up our shining iron towers.
The people came here
From all around the world,
And what is it all for,
But the right to belly-ache?
The rich don't understand the poor,
So they hate them.
The poor don't understand the rich,
So they hate them too.
We, the people and all the people,
The Earth groans under our footprints.
Society is a contagion on this planet
And we are not so good as the horned beast.
For it does not cry for wealth nor forgiveness,
But there is nothing a goat hates more
Than another goat.

Blue Law

Most businesses were closed on Sundays.
This was not a topic on the national news
Nor a conversation around the supper table.
On Sundays, people didn't mow their lawns
Nor paint their houses.
There was an unspoken shame in these activities.
The non-church-goer could piddle in the garage
Or go fishing.

It was possible to get a loaf of bread
And a pack of cigarettes on Sunday.
Most towns had a 24-hour truck stop.
If your car gave you trouble,
You could call the mechanic
Because you knew his number.
People didn't carry lists.
The numbers were memorized.
If you couldn't remember a number,
You simply gave a shout out.
Someone close by would recite it for you.

Gas stations were full-service.
Motorists would simply pull into the bay
And a friendly attendant would scuttle
Out to your car. A customer could
Simply hand him a twenty
And say "fill 'er up."
As the gas was being pumped
The windshield would be washed.
After the tank was filled and gas cap secured,
The attendant would scuttle back inside
To get your change.

Remembering way, way back

When I was a kid
We hid dimes in our shoes;
There were holes in our pockets.
We rambled the streets unsupervised.
Momma would give each of us a dime
To call home in case of incident.
At least one kid had to wear shoes
So someone could carry the dimes.
In the evenings,
The coins were returned
To Momma's change purse.

So, what did dimes have to do with phones?
We used phone booths to make calls.
Phone booths were glass closets
That stood on street corners
And in front of grocery stores.
We stepped inside a booth and
Closed the glass door.

There was a big metal box in the booth.
The metal box was the actual telephone.
Remove the handset from the metal box,
Drop one dime in the upper coin slot,
Punch in the number you were trying to reach.
A quarter was required for a long-distance call.
If the connection was not completed,
The coins would be returned in the lower drawer
After hanging up the handset.

Social media was writing a note
On a piece of paper,
Folding it into a football,
Flicking it across the classroom
To your buddy.

Back in my day
We didn't have air conditioning,
Unless you special ordered it
For a new home.
Most of us just toughed it out
By sitting in front of a fan
Or in the shade during the afternoon.
There weren't very many fat kids.
You could easily pick him out of a crowd
Because he wasn't in the crowd.
He was sitting over there by himself,
On the curb, sweating.

Back in my day,
Kids got their asses spanked in the store.
Cars didn't have seat belts
And we didn't have car seats neither.
The very idea of the government
Telling us how to raise our children!
When kids were little,
They were simply stuffed in the seat
Between the adults.
By the time they were in the second grade
They were old enough
To ride in the back of the truck.
There was usually a gun rack
In the rear window of the truck.
And rifles were carried on them too.
That's the way it was and we liked it.

The Hunter's Den

Feel winters' brisk air rolling in?
Oh, hunting season's here!
Let's clean our guns and pack our things.
It's time to shoot a deer.

We'll gather at the hunting den
Way down the logging trail.
Five miles to camp at forest's end
With lonesome whippoorwill.

The den still stands among the oaks.
The wooden floor boards creak.
It smells of jerky and of smoke.
The roof it doesn't leak.

A musket hangs above the door,
The wall, a buckskin hide.
A bear rug lays across the floor
To welcome us inside.

An old black stove to warm our bones,
The firewood neatly stacked.
And copper kettles in a row
On metal pantry rack.

Let's put the deer stand on the tree.
Oh, hunting season's here!
Let's sharpen knives and brew coffee
For soon we'll shoot a deer.

Our time to hunt deep in the wild.
We're here to stay the week.
Old cots with woolen blankets piled,
Iron pans to fry our meat.

So many heads of great horned beasts,
They tell of days gone by,
Are mounted high upon the eaves
Where dust grows on their eyes.

We'll share a sip of honey ale
And then it's off to bed
To dream of bouncing pure white tail
Deer dancing in our heads.

Take Me with You

If you go downtown early morning
You can see the shopkeepers setting
Old treasures on the sidewalk,
Writing their welcomes with chalk
On little standing blackboards,
Inviting you inside their stores.

Honeysuckle Antiques has its window
Filled with newfound things to show,
Local crafts and the latest junk,
A fringed lampshade and leather trunks.
Its storefront arranged with trifle clutter,
Metal lawn chairs and wooden ladders.

A rusted garden rake's crooked grin
Begs you to come shop within.
A copper cowbell rings above the door
As dust scurries across a creaking floor.
Greetings from a curvy dressmaker's bodice,
Empty coke bottles sold by the case.

The moment you enter you're lost in time.
You never know what you may find;
A stack of old suitcases eager to travel,
Tiny dishes all the way from China,
A basket full of skeleton keys
Or an old black Singer sewing machine.

So many things lost and forgotten;
A lady's hat pin, hundreds of buttons
Peer through the green glass of Mason jars,
A boy's prize collection of toy metal cars,
Polaroid cameras and a reel to reel,
A pair of broken red wagon wheels.

Everyone's favorite, a brown Teddy bear,
A no-longer-needed baby high chair,
Piles of silver spoons, a tarnished pocket watch;
Its workings inside have ground to a halt.
Someone's keepsake once shiny and new,
Time of death; twelve thirty-two.

Overhead, a beautiful lead chandelier
Sparkles "I don't belong here.
Take me with you when you go."
Shelves lined with items needing a home.
Cramped, dusty isles you wander around
Through all the lost and all the found.

Then persuasive orphans catch your eye;
A porcelain doll sitting way up high,
Sad, in her torn and faded dress
Next to some pink Depression glass.
"Take me with you when you go."
Beg the doll and the bowl.

I Followed the Sun

Friends may come and friends may go.
Be happy. Let God's love warm your face.
Follow the sun.

Help me carry the heavy load.
Be alive! There's plenty of dreams to chase.
Friends may come and friends may go.

Show me love on the lonely road.
Be kind, even though your heart will break.
Just follow the sun.

Give me a hand, someone to hold.
Be in love! There's plenty of love to make.
Friends may come and friends may go.

Come with me. Let's build a home.
Be patient. We will find us a place.
We'll follow the sun.

Give me hope when I grow old.
Be at peace. Give me His saving grace.
Friends may come, friends may go.
I followed the sun.

Sisters

Many days were spent
On the veranda dressing reluctant kittens
In doll clothes and bonnets.
The backyard stretched
To the edge of Shaky Bib's holler
Where the big catalpa stood.
Sometimes we would sneak off
To the treehouse, anxious to escape
Beyond the touch of everyday world.
We would gather wildflowers
And weave them into crowns
With long strands of Johnson grass.
All day we lolled about
In the treehouse like queens,
Proclaiming our rein over any
Who passed nearby. At last,
When the sun burned orange in the west
And long shadows grew eastward,
We would begin our way home,
Stopping by the creek
To toss our woven jewels
And watch them float away.

Dear Passenger

I hoped to find you this morning
Standing beneath the desert sky.
The stage coach is gone.
I'm looking down the road.
Oh, if you had chosen
Me to be your only one.
Is anybody going to Nevada?

I hoped to see you this morning
Dressed in Sunday best and tie.
Didn't think you'd really leave.
Left me standing in the street.
Sitting on the pew alone.
The stage coach is gone.
Is anybody going to Nevada?

Heavenly Father,

Thank you for accepting me for who I am.
In spite of all my weaknesses and failures,
You are always there for me.
Help me to always be humble, open to correction,
And teachable so that I may learn and grow.

In Jesus' name, Amen.

The Essential Miss Meow-Meow

Perched upon the upholstered chair
This sable brute smugly bathes,
Admiring her slender physique
In the morning sun,
Murmurs, stretches and yawns.

Her tender pads land the floor
With the slightest thud. Then
Slinking from room to room
Rubbing on the baseboards
This inhabitant of the hallways.

With visceral, jittering whiskers
She commits her crimes in broad day
Not of burning rage nor hunger
But innate skill and grace
This murderous and masterful creature.

Two amber eyes in a fearful silhouette,
A mouth full of white daggers,
The mouse is not her foe
No more than a scratching post:
A tasty treat, the lily's nectar.

Two tiny black beads unblinking,
The rodent's stench lay balanced
On the tip of her tongue with anticipation.
One choking pounce, piercing the sinews
A fish hook in the eye.

A fatal burst upon violent slinging
One short squeal resonating outward
Two quick beats and then fail
The arms lay wide open to the air
No moaning for release.

Tuttle Mountain

Once there was a boy
And we would climb Tuttle Mountain
Right up to the very peak,
Where only lovers went.

Persuaded by a northern wind
And lonesome coos of mourning dove.
A changing weather convinced me
To collaborate with my younger self;

I chose the old path upward,
Once used by many for inspiration,
To see the artist's overlook
And make the climb all by my lone.

Oh how I wished to fly away,
To be fearless of finding Earth again,
Where morning mist hugs the mountain side;
Forgotten places I've long since been.

As I reflected on my wayward youth
The day hung low in murky state.
It begged me witness the dismal sun.
I walked on at the wind's command.

Past the tender garden mead
Brown with drupes of dying seed,
Treading leaves deep underfoot
And happy in my leather boots.

Upward through jagged and bony trees
I climbed the hill.
It was easier then, for I used his will,
But that boy is long gone now.

Not remembering the grade to be so steep
And he's not here to hold my hand
Or help me cross the rough terrain.
My mind's eye sketched his gentle face.

What present things required of me
Or treasures found with day so dull?
Should I progress and further go
To gain top ground and climb the knoll?

And then the sky began to break
Behind thick clouds, the sun protest.
An eagle's view revealed to me
O'er spacious fields all cattle flecked.

A vantage point to my delight;
The patchwork fields of countryside
Were stitched into the rural tapestry
Where lawns of sloping land recedes.

Below, the endless hedgerow boundaries
Around green velvet naps in harmony.
A farmer, slow moving on his plow
To cut and comb the braided rows.

And saltbox chimneys caught my eye,
Blue scrolls of smoke build and pile.
The twinkling kitchen lights displayed
Across the valley miles away.

And then I stood and touched the sky
Upon that Tuttle Mountain high.
My heart was filled with confidence
To turn and make the long descent.

Lawnmower Therapy

I drove into town today
To get a burger and a shake.
I said no mustard when I paid,
But I got mustard anyway.

I don't really give a hoot,
Old cut-off jeans and cowboy boots.
It's all on my side of the fence.
Don't give a dang 'bout fashion sense.

Let's get on out and mow.
Need time to search my soul.
Lawnmower therapy
Lawnmower therapy

Let's put this puppy into gear,
A cigarette and ice cold beer.
I woke up with bad news today,
My boy, Tom Petty passed away.

A mass shooting in Las Vegas,
I don't know what's become of us.
It's five years Momma's in the grave
Almost exactly to the day.

Had to turn off the news.
It's giving me the blues.
Lawnmower therapy
Lawnmower therapy

I'll cut this whole ten-acre field.
I need a little time to heal.
The Puerto Rico hurricane,
Maria wiped it all away.

Oh, country folk, they understand.
Don't need no one to lend a hand.
I'll shoot the grass right in your face
If you don't get clear of my space.

I wanna mow the lawn,
Sing a really sad, sad song.
Lawnmower therapy
Lawnmower therapy

I put away the phone.
Don't bother me, nobody's home.
Lawnmower therapy
I'll ride into the sun,
Sing an old sad, sad song.
Lawnmower therapy

There is still a little gas.
I think I'll make another pass
And drink another brew,
Sing an old sad, sad tune.

I don't care what you say.
I need a little time to pray.
Lawnmower therapy
Lawnmower therapy

Say Goodbye

The last blooms of summer have put on a show.
Long hot days and cloudless afternoons
Have led to wooly side yards left unmowed.
Woody stems holding bright yellow blooms

High above the rest like flags on a pole.
The roadsides dress in long ruffled skirts.
Hear the flowers yelling from the fencerows?
Why are they here, toiling in the dirt?

Miles of rank weeds and stubborn wildflowers
Scattered about and crying of thirst.
Lines of the curly cup gumweed tower;
Bright yellow from the damp ditches burst.

Tall swaying beside the crackling pavement,
Roots held tight in hardened fists of dirt.
They are the last of summer's arrangements.
See thousands of yellow petals flirt?

You, in the motorcar, hear them shouting,
Smiling, winking and looking so fine,
Raising a ruckus and being rowdy?
Soon autumn's blush will leave them behind.

Ecclesiastes 12:8

Be not perplexed on all
That belongs to this earthly life
For a door opens wide before man
In his hour of death.

Because the poet was wise
He tried to teach knowledge
And sought out many
Acceptable words of truth.

But the poet was just a bookmaker
Pricking the hearts of men
To do good labor in the fields.
He was a thief and a robber
From the one Good Shepherd.

He grew weary
By the study of many sayings.
Finding in conclusion
The whole duty of man: Fear God
And keep His commandments.

The Cattleman

It's sundown on the open range;
All day in pastures green.
There's not a thing he wants to change.
He's tired but he is free.

The cows are swatting with their tails
And chewing on their cud.
His camp is far from wheel-worn trail.
He's brought a little food.

He picks his teeth with pocket knife
While night bugs sing their song.
So happy with the cowboy life;
A fire to keep him warm.

He stirs the embers in his fire,
Enjoys some jerked beef.
The shadows hide his hard, dark eyes;
Held in by large crow's feet.

His big mustache tries not to swear,
To live by cowboy code;
Be honest, true and always fair,
Be proud but not too bold.

A saddle placed beneath his head,
God's grace upon his soul.
Tonight the earth will be his bed
As stars put on a show.

The Forgotten Garden

I came across a lonesome property
When on return from county seat
To clear myself of taxes due
And claim my yearly revenue.
My horse was fresh from farrier.
The good mare had fallen into stride.
The musty coach in need of wear
And so I let Old Gypsy decide.

The narrow lane split from the road
And wound along the old peach groves.
We excused ourselves from vulgarity
And busy town folk savagery.
So not to waste a day in June,
No need to hurry home so soon,
We took the old orchard road
And dreamt of peaches on the groves.

But as we came on down the lane,
I found the farm was not the same.
With fruit stand closed and tightly sealed,
Young cattle grazed the orchard fields.
The pristine house, a vacant property
That once gleamed of prosperity.
Even the mare slowed to a trot
To see the orchards lay in rot.

I knew nothing of the residents.
The box no longer wore a name.
Being no more than common stock,
I knew not their whereabouts
Nor details of their circumstance.
The wind had tossed the realtor's sign.
Unread papers rotted on the drive.
My mind was lost in backward glance.

No coachman in the parking bay
Nor butler at the entry way.
The blinds were all pulled tightly shut.
A ragged lawn was left uncut.
The house comprised of fairest stones
By skillful hands for longevity.
The timbers inside held firm and strong
From years of loving husbandry.

I felt a pinch of bitterness
For the neighboring hills and dales
That so graciously donated thus.
A lavish farm left to assails,
But stately oaks enclosed the lawn,
And redbuds placed among them there.
A narrow side yard held intrigue
With hosts of cosmos gone to seed.

Woody mums grew thin and tall
Beside a stone retaining wall.
The footpath was healed and needed wear.
Fair trellises fell in despair.
At pathway's end, the rotten handle of a rake
And a hoe leaned against the garden gate,
Someone had thought to barricade
With stacks of upturned pots of clay.

Ashamedly, I lingered for a while
Considering the effort to clear the stile.
Surrendering to adventure's propense,
I decided then to jump the fence.
With sadness, I'll tell what I found.
Dried bouquets lie on the ground;
Once red bows on a Christmas spray,
Concealed behind a rusted gate.

A splendid court with all its bowers
That once smelled sweet with drooping flowers.
Today, a neglected bit of real estate
With herbs of summer all gone astray,
To lie with weeds beyond their borders
In unkempt habit of disorder.
The rose hip that once was heavy laden,
Now petals' shed and bees' abandon.

Old customs left here unpreserved.
The grindstone no longer turned.
Nothing moved but the black bird's eye
In this static summer place.
A sun dial no longer told the time
For a lichen beard grew on its face.
Tired lilies lost their aspiration;
Dried memorials in the flower bed.

In yesteryear, an estate promoted
In the balance of excess and frugal.
Simply a virtuous country life
That boasts nothing artificial.
But time grew on with determination,
Whispering names of the dead.
And ne'er a stray dog wanders by;
A rough stone marker of family pet.

At this nostalgic and forgotten place
All the garden lay perfectly still,
Unconcerned by my thoughts
Of living here, on this orchard estate
As one of its wholesome, honored guests.
With no hospitalities spared
And merry hosts from ancient families
With behaviors that should be encouraged.

The lady of all her manner and grace;
Good neighbors came to taste her ware.
Pies cooling in the window sill
And fine silver had the cupboards filled.
Her guests were every pleasantry shown;
Embraced this proper country home.
For everyone was invited by a single bell.
Staff and master dined on the same bird.

For fertile soil yields such benefit.
No crime for distinction from the rest.
The lady embodied all forms of modesty,
Like other good country wives.
Unspoiled and steeped in innocence,
A mindful gardener of great wealth
In younger years and better health.
The birds came just to please her.

I did not contest their ownership
For they were distinguished, indeed
And regarded as such.
Not by want of enterprise,
But of a simple country life
Where goodness is married to pleasure.
I could have stayed a century there
At that humble orchard estate.

Then my mare began to stammer
And my watch told me to travel on.
So, to the orchard road we took
Past rolling hills of tender fruit.
My chest grew tight as tenterhooks
And reins pulled straight by jolly horse.
Sweet peaches hanging on the groves,
Glad pastures left to lay untamed.

The Last One

One morning in the market place
I met a man with contorted face.
A full grown man, mature in years,
His eyes were red and full of tears.

When his face looked unto mine
He turned away and tried to hide.
Embarrassed by some unknown crime,
A baby goat tucked at his side.

I asked the man "Why do you weep?"
He wiped his tears upon his sleeve.
"The blame lies with this little goat,
And sadness has ruined my coat."

I asked "What could this small thing do
To make your temperament so blue?"
He stammered and with a guttural start
Laid his sorrow on my heart.

"Today I fetched him from the barn.
He was the last one on my farm.
I've raised these things since in my youth,
For all my life, I can't refute."

"I got the first ones as a boy.
From them, I raised a plenty more.
Soon, in my charge, a lovely herd,
Kept by watchful eye and kindly word."

"Through breed and trade my stock increased.
The line, I carefully policed."
The man broke up and smiled with shame.
"Each nanny had a given name."

"And then, some years I took a spouse.
No sooner than the moment wed,
The focus, on things of the house,
And scarcely knew my flock were fed."

"For I was rich with worries few.
My love for her was still brand new.
Over time, we had many kids.
I speak now of the two-legged kind."

"New books and clothes to wear to school.
My wife, she wanted fancy jewels.
I sold an old one here and there.
The weathers went without a care."

"The herd it shrank with little thought.
Lo! The whimsical things I bought.
Then hard times found me not so wealthy.
I sold to spare my children poverty."

"Besides, the herd was good and healthy,
Which numbered then at more than fifty.
But numbers shrank and woe to me,
The line, it dwindled down to thirty."

"But one by one they met our needs,
And served us in our wicked deeds.
For me, it was our darkest days
To see my goat herd melt away."

"The numbers slipped from ten to four,
From four to three and three to two.
For what was fifty, now only one
Asleep here on my very arm."

Then I proclaimed "For heaven's sake!"
"I think my very heart will break.
This crime, you've done it to yourself.
The blame it lies with no one else."

"I'll buy this young one here and now.
You wipe those tears from off your brow.
And keep your goat then be the miser,
Lest no one here should be the wiser."

"Young man," he fussed "I did not come for charity!
What kind of person would I be?
The kid is yours. You paid me true.
You make me out to be a fool."

I begged the old man go home to sleep
For I'm the fool –To buy a goat I do not keep.
With that, he winked and turned for home,
The little goat tucked in his arms.

www.ingramcontent.com/pod-product-compliance
Ingram Content Group UK Ltd.
Pitfield, Milton Keynes, MK11 3LW, UK
UKHW041920190726
13854UKWH00003B/1348

9 781387 314201